Pitcher Full
of Prayers

Taylor K. Arthur

Blessings, Merideth!

Taylor K Arthur

DEDICATION

This book is dedicated to the two women who raised me up on prayer: my mother, Nanette, whose morning prayers beside the sliding glass window ingrained in me the importance of meeting with Jesus first thing, and my Grandma Afton, whose steadfast devotion to prayer inspired three generations to love and serve Jesus. I am who I am because of both your prayers. I love you.

CONTENTS

Foreword:
Where's the Cheer Section?

And as for you . . . sisters, never tire of doing what is good.
2 Thessalonians 3:13

I am blessed with a family who shows up in full-force for sporting events, award ceremonies, and graduations. They boom and scream, even when they're not supposed to. They bring bullhorns. It. Is. Awesome. Even as a teenager feigning a "too cool for school" attitude when they erupted into applause, I secretly delighted in my crazy cheer section.

Something funny happened after I became a mom, though. After all of those years of awards ceremonies and graduations, followed by bridal showers, a wedding, then a baby shower, the baby came home.

Bleeding nipples, sleep deprivation, sleep walking through diaper changes, navigating a breast pump torture device, and loving a husband who may sympathize and help but cannot replace me, paled every other work I had ever done. I looked around me in shock, realizing for the first time that this is the work of motherhood: backbreaking, torturous joy on repeat, day in and day out.

Pouring myself into this tiny being who sleeps and spits up and fills his pants without a care, who never seems to be particularly grateful, is the deepest, most raw giving I have ever done. I stare at him nursing in the midnights, rock him until he burps, tears running at the marvel of a love so much bigger and harder than anyone could have ever explained to me. I marvel at how I am being pushed through this sieve of motherhood, my selfish nature stripping away, my orders of importance tossed and rearranged into this child's wellbeing. I burp him, lay him in his bed. I crawl under the covers and watch my husband sleep deeply (really?), and wonder if there is anyone else awake in the whole dark night right now. I smile as I try to fall asleep, confident there is another mama out there doing the exact same thing at this weary moment.

So where are the cheer sections? After all, there is more grit in breastfeeding through one bout of mastitis than any AP exam I ever sat for. Why aren't there cheer sections everywhere, complete with bullhorns and "Way to Go, Mom!" signs, following moms around throughout their days?

I listen for the cheer section sometimes. But no clapping audience erupts spontaneously in the midnights. There is no cheer section in the kitchen when my heart baby throws up all the milk I've pumped for him along with all of his meds. There is no "Way to Go" sign in the hospital room at 5am when he wakes me up to restart Dumbo again. No one applauds me in this deep, naked work of mothering. I stand in their room at night after a rub-you-raw day, and I wonder if I'm doing this right. I kneel and I pray; I cry and I beg for grace. Mostly, I pray I won't screw them up.

Morning keeps coming, and exhaustion shuffles down the hall alongside me as I make my way to their bedrooms. I squint at day filtering through the curtains, cruel and harsh, until I see the sun rising in their faces, bursting with delight at the sight of me. Me: tired, sieved, broken, greasy-haired, who loses her temper and shrieks like a banshee and hides in the bathroom when she just needs a minute of peace. Me, who used to knot at the sound of a baby crying because I have never wanted anything—anyone—more.

"Mama!" That's what they call me as I pull them out of their beds. They cling gratefully, and I inhale their little boy smells, their first words of the day, their still-smallness. Exhaustion slinks back down the hallway as my two rising sons fling joy wide across my world. There are no plastic gold trophies, no bullhorns, in this little boys' nursery. No one will remember how many times I woke up with them last night. And yet, I'd trade every shiny affirmation in the world for their beaming faces. They wrap around me like a couple of koala bears, and I maneuver down the stairs cloaked in chubby arms and luscious kisses. Who needs a cheer section, anyways?

This book is meant to be a little cheer section for you, a little piece of comfort you can pack around in your purse or your diaper bag and pull out when you need a moment of encouragement. There are just enough entries—thirty-one—to get you through a month, if you want to look at it that way.

This book is a great follow up to the "Pitcher Talk," and if you've seen it, you'll know exactly what I'm talking about. It progresses through the levels of the pitcher needs, so the first entries deal with basic needs, then safety needs, relationship needs, esteem needs, up to the last entries focusing on purpose. If you're working on filling up your pitcher, this little book of prayers will help you do just that.

As you read this little book of prayers, I pray that your heart will be especially blessed in the hours of mamahood, in the midnights and early mornings, especially on your rub-you-raw days. May this book bless you and serve as a well to fill your pitcher so that your own heart will be filled to the brim with joy and overflow love and kindness to your family.

Love,
Taylor

My Story

I was twenty-one years old when a doctor I had never met before explained to me that I had bipolar disorder and that I would be on a mood stabilizer for the rest of my life. As I stood there in hospital scrubs, half-awake and fully drugged on my first dose of lithium, there was only one question I could think to ask, "Can I still be a mother?"

It took six years for me to become stable enough for my team of doctors to finally agree to partner with me through a bipolar pregnancy. After a very healthy pregnancy, we were devastated to lose our first baby boy, Caleb Joshua, to heaven at 36 weeks. We waited another 15 months to hold our rainbow baby, Abraham, in our arms. And then, just 26 months later, after being told he would not survive the pregnancy because of his special heart, Samuel, "Sam-kicker" was born alive. He spent two and a half weeks in the NICU at Seattle Children's before he came home to grow up and be our boy.

Our family now lives in Puyallup, WA. The boys are growing and thriving. We continue to accompany Samuel on his heart journey, step on Legos, celebrate Caleb's memory, and live out our twisted, blissful life. Jack and I both work at home. I get to speak to MOPS groups and churches about mental wellness while blogging and writing, volunteering in the boys' school, going on walks, and planting as many flowers in the yard. You can follow our story at taylorkarthur.com.

Dear Lord,
I bring You all of my most
basic needs:
my family's need for shelter,
food, clothing, health, and wellbeing.
I bring you my need for
sleep & rest, time to take care of myself,
a new outfit,
for simple alone time and breathing space.
I know you can supply all of my needs,
Jesus.
I trust You.
Amen

1.
First Thing

*But seek first his kingdom and his righteousness, and all these
things will be given to you as well.*
Matthew 6:33

My morning holy routine required my utmost attention
every morning, no matter what. Since childhood, I imagined
God downstairs impatiently tapping his fingers, waiting for
me to get my lazy butt out of bed. He required me to wake up
early and read my Bible, write in my journal, and spend at
least a good half an hour with Him before every one in the
house awoke. Fitting my "God time" into the to-do list was
something I needed to do every day in order to feel good
about my life.

But everything changed when I started therapy and my
therapist made me promise I would start working on getting
enough sleep. I could not get up early anymore. What would
God do without me in the mornings? I couldn't imagine not
having my Bible time, but I desperately needed the sleep.

Morning after morning, as I woke up more and more
rested, I was surprised to realize God was still there to greet
me, even if it was just for a quick prayer at the foot of my
bed. I realized that the God who made me to sleep and said I
was "very good" was not downstairs judging me because I
was sleeping in. Maybe, instead, He was happy I was finally
taking care of myself?

So now, I see my God time a little differently. My first
moment with Him doesn't have to be rigmarole of Bible study
or perfectly worded prayer. It can be a quiet, "Morning,
Papa," or a smile upward, a prayer in my heart. To Him, it all
means the same as long as He and I connect.

3

The first thing is not a task. Nor is the first thing an obligation. The first thing is my right. The first thing is what I was born for.

You see, I am the child of the King. And so are you. We belong in His arms, at His feet, whispering prayers into his ears first thing. We belong in His presence first thing because this moment, face-to-face, cheek-to-cheek, with our Father keeps us connected to His version of our story.

He is my first thing because He reminds me who I am. I remember every day in my first moments with Him that my story is much bigger than today's troubles. My definition is bigger than wife, mother, writer, housekeeper. My definition, my purpose, is eternal. I am His, first thing.

I've stopped looking at morning quiet time as a task to complete. Sometimes I read my Bible, sometimes I don't. Sometimes I sing, and sometimes I cry into my coffee cup. But I say good morning to my Daddy, no matter what, whether I have an hour for a Bible study or a moment for a quick prayer. Because He's my first thing.

May He be yours.

Lord Jesus, please help me to find you first in my days, to order my days in such a way that I give honor to the body you have given me and call very good. I praise you for your constant presence in my life and loving kindness. Amen.

2.
Waiting Upon the Lord

But those who hope in the Lord
will renew their strength.
They will soar on wings like eagles;
they will run and not grow weary,
they will walk and not be faint.
Isaiah 40:31

I have been waiting for a long time. I have been waiting for pay day, I have been waiting to graduate, to get married, to be healthy, to have a baby, to be done nursing, to get back to my pre-baby weight . . . I have waited and waited and waited.

I didn't even realize how much waiting I had done until Sam was given to us. All of those waitings seemed so silly in light of the new adventure of waiting we began when he was only 19 weeks in utero. We waited two more weeks for a diagnosis, then we waited for him to go into heart failure. We waited for the next doctor's opinion, and then for the next appointment. I waited in the delivery room as they examined him in the NICU after he was born. We waited two and half more weeks in the NICU before he could come home.

There was a moment when I was pregnant with Sam, as I was driving up to the hospital for one of so many tests, when I realized my life couldn't be about waiting anymore. There was no "until" with Sam. I didn't want to wait until he was better or until—what? He didn't have a heart condition? I realized that I didn't want Sam's journey to be about untils.

Our life was going to be a series of untils, framed by doctor's appointments, or an entirely new kind of journey. I

5

had to learn a new way of viewing my life in a new context: one in which our joy and peace could be constant in the midst of an undisclosed waiting period.

Would we waste Sam's life being consumed with fear? He was alive, kicking inside me, and I had to figure out how that moment could be enough. I had to stop waiting and start living, start living out every moment of my life so that if this day and this moment was the only life my child would ever know, it would be spent in joy and peace and love.

In that moment I realized that this waiting is a problem, maybe even a sickness in my own heart. Why did I think I could wait until? Why did I ever think that the culmination of one set of circumstances would ever lead to my fulfillment? For every hurdle, every mountain climbed or waited out, there was another. Every horizon begets another horizon, and I am forever chasing, waiting.

Isaiah 40:31 is so familiar to me, so comforting. And yet, I have wondered my entire life what it meant to wait upon the Lord. I knew what it was to love the Lord, worship, praise, and thank the Lord. I knew what it was to trust the Lord. But to "wait on Him"? And so it was as I drove up I-5 with my big pregnant belly and the praise music blasting that Isaiah 43:31 penetrated deep into the marrow of my understanding:

They that wait upon the LORD shall renew their strength; they shall mount up with wings as eagles; they shall run, and not be weary; and they shall walk, and not faint . . .

Waiting upon the LORD my God means to be constantly, fervently, deliberately, waiting for Him to appear in each and every one of my life circumstances. Am I looking for Him, right now, to fill every need I have? Am I asking him to be present when I am at the grocery store and

I can't quite fill my complete list with the amount of money in my checking account? Do I trust him when the safe neighborhood we moved into starts to decline? Can I trust him when I total the car and there is no money to replace it? When the perfect job ends up being a dead end? When the people we thought we could build a business with turn out to not share our values at all? Am I putting all of my beliefs and all of my hope into Man's predictions, actions, or opinions? Who is in control of my life, after all: doctors, bankers, employers, oppressors . . . or God?

Spending a life running from paycheck to paycheck, from appointment to appointment, from person to person is exhausting, an infinite mountain range. But what if instead of running the gamut of my life's circumstances, I just wait for Him to come? What if I just sit, and trust, and believe that His Glory will flood this circumstance, and the next? What if I wait for an indwelling that fills me so fully that I can scale the mountains, face the fear and the pain and the emptiness, already satiated?

Whoa. And there it is: being a Christian won't dismiss me from engaging life. But if I am filled—every crack and cranny, crevice and craving—with the indwelling of the Most High, what I face on earth is but one small piece of my reality. I am facing this trial, but I am swimming in glory. I am climbing the mountain, but He is renewing my strength.

What are you waiting on? Join me in asking God to fill our yearnings with His glory.

Lord, thank you for always being faithful to walk beside me in every one of my moments of need. There is nothing I can want for, nothing I can cry out to you for that you haven't already foreseen. I pray that you will fill me and give me strength to mount up with wings like eagles and rise above

these earthly troubles.
I trust you, Lord, to fill me and strengthen me. Amen.

3.
Prayer Over the Pantry

*For every animal of the forest is mine, and the cattle on a
thousand hills.*
Psalm 50:10

Lord, I'm placing my hands on this pantry
In the quiet of this kitchen right now.
Do You see me?
The calendar seems to stand still
As this budget slips through my fingers.
I can't. Quite. Hold on.
I feel this quake deep in my gut.
I want to run scared,
Fill the shelves with my panic.
But then I hear You whisper,
I've got you.
And I know you've got the cattle,
I know you grow the wheat.
I know you break two loaves and pass five fishes
Feed five thousand and fill baskets to spare.
So I'm standing in this kitchen.
I'm placing my hands on this pantry.
And I'm trusting You.
Amen.

4.
Choosing Right Now

"but few things are needed—or indeed only one . . ."
Luke 10:42

The rose garden blooms pink and gangly outside the dining room window this summer morning. Sam screams at the kids' table, two hours after I've served breakfast, naked from the waist down, refusing. Abraham traces the word "big," practicing sight words for kindergarten. The details of a day feel more like an ever-heightening Everest: the cleaning of house and folding of laundry, tutoring 5- year-old in alphabets and numbers, forming the will of 2-year-old-breakfast-refuser, the making of lunch and planning of dinner, finding time to blog, making phone calls to pharmacies and doctors' offices. 10 am feels tired. I sag at the sink, still full of dishes I swear I've washed once already this morning.

Sam carefully climbs off his bench where he has been fitting for the last two hours. He picks up his breakfast bowl and tilts it to show me he has finished his oatmeal. I affirm him, feeling barely the victor after this battle of wills, "Thank you, Sam."

Bare booty and legs jiggle in a happy dance over to the counter where he places his bowl, turns around with hands raised, and shouts, "I win!"

Could you help but laugh? Win what? He doesn't care. He's accomplished the task before him, and even if his pride and stubbornness contributed to him struggling with something as simple as sitting still and eating his breakfast, even if he is the one making it hard on himself this morning, he still wins when he reaches his goal. He still wins.

I wonder if that is what is going on with me. I pile

enormous amounts of pressure on myself over simple things. God's given me a task for this moment. Instead of just doing it, I make it so hard. I sit and fit for hours over something simple. I try to get up and run around. I make more lists of things I should be doing. In actuality, it is more simple than I ever really imagined. Even after all of this time, I'm still trying to live outside the boundaries of my life. I'm trying to give outside my own ability, to find the sweet spot between stretching myself just a little further and crashing. I have an endless list of expectations of myself; I think most of us moms do. But God maybe doesn't. Maybe God just wants us to sit down and eat our breakfast. He wants me to sit down and do the one thing right in front of me, the ONE thing I am called to.

Jesus told Martha, as she ran around and resented her sister Mary,

"Martha, Martha," the Lord answered, "you are worried and upset about many things, but few things are needed—or indeed only one" (Luke 10:41-42).

Only one thing? I have been thinking about this all day and I am still confused. How, my Martha spirit frustrates, is it possible to ever do one thing in this mothering life of mine? How do I ever just get to focus on one face without tallying the grocery list? How do I ever get to cook dinner without my two year old pulling my skirt over his head?

Lord, with all due respect, I feel for Martha. And for me. And I think you're being a little harsh, don't you think?

But then, as I push through Target and pick out bacon at the grocery store, as I drive in the driveway and look at the front porch that is still a littered disaster, as I rush outside to kiss a pricked finger, I begin to wonder that maybe the one thing isn't what I think. Maybe the one thing is simply this present moment. And whether I'm kneeling in prayer or scrubbing the kitchen floor, whether I'm wiping a nose or

11

writing a blog, Jesus is in this moment. My one thing is right now; my one thing is always now.

Now is the only place Jesus resides, the only place I can touch eternity. Now deserves reverence and attention and a little bit of wonder.

Right now it's cooling off and husband just finished work for the day. Right now, he's out there swinging my babies high in the swing tree: the tree we cuddle under during lunchtime and stare through to blue, wrapped up in sticky peanut butter kisses and hugs. Right now is my only thing: my Jesus, my salvation, all that really exists.

So, I choose reverence. I choose my one thing: now. Oh, soul, how many times must you learn this?

Lord, I pray that you will help me to focus on this moment that you are giving me right now. Help me not to worry about the next thing that I might have to do, but to truly see the beauty that you are offering me in this very minute. Thank you so much that you are unveiling yourself moment by moment and that I can trust you to never stop giving Yourself to me. Amen.

5.

Hagar's Prayer

So [Sarah] said to Abraham, "Drive out this slave with her
son, for the son of this slave will not be a coheir with my son
Isaac!" Now this was a very difficult thing for Abraham
because of his son. But God said to Abraham, "Do not be
concerned about the boy and your slave. Whatever Sarah
says to you, listen to her, because your offspring will be
traced through Isaac. But I will also make a nation of the
slave's son because he is your offspring."
Early in the morning Abraham got up, took bread and a
water skin, put them on Hagar's shoulders, and sent her and
the boy away. She left and wandered in the Wilderness of
Beer-Sheba. When the water in the skin was gone, she left
the boy under one of the bushes. Then she went and sat
down nearby, about a bowshot away, for she said, "I can't
bear to watch the boy die!" So as she sat nearby, she wept
loudly.
God heard the voice of the boy, and the angel of God called
to Hagar from heaven and said to her, "What's wrong,
Hagar? Don't be afraid, for God has heard the voice of the
boy from the place where he is. Get up, help the boy up, and
support him, for I will make him a great nation." Then God
opened her eyes, and she saw a well of water. So she went
and filled the water skin and gave the boy a drink. God was
with the boy, and he grew; he settled in the wilderness and
became an archer. He settled in the Wilderness of Paran,
and his mother got a wife for him from the land of Egypt.
Genesis 21:10-21

Dear Lord,
We offer up the children we carry.
As mothers, you built us inside and out to carry our babies.

13

Sometimes this carrying exhausts to despair.
Have you forgotten us, out in the desert,
thrown away for others You favor more?
But that is not who we know You to be.
You call us forgotten ones "Ishmael," and "Samuel."
You name our children "God has heard"
so that every day in the desert we know:
We Are Yours.
When all is lost, you send messengers.
When we thirst, a well appears.
How precious to me are your thoughts, God! How vast is the
sum of them! Were I to count them, they would outnumber
the grains of sand—when I awake, I am still with you.
We offer our children up to their real Father,
and we pray for peace.
We pray for wells in the desert to drink from,
to watch and marvel at your provision
while we raise Your wilderness children.
Glory be to you alone.
Amen.

6.
Rest Deep in His Shelter

He will cover you with his feathers. He will shelter you with
his wings. His faithful promises are your armor and
protection.
Psalm 91:4

We all have days when we could use some extra shelter.
Maybe you just saw a picture of yourself at your kids'
school's 80's themed auction and realized that really wasn't
the best choice of costume. Or, maybe that's just me.

Maybe you're sitting in a hospital room, next to your
sick baby or your sick mama, feeling helpless and
wondering what to do next. Maybe you're waiting for news
that will change everything or for someone to tell you
whether you're in or you're out. Maybe you're just feeling
like you need an extra layer of protection before you head
out into a world that doesn't explain, doesn't include,
forgets, runs late, and then forgets to call. Maybe you just
need someone to put their arms around you and tell you, *you*
know? I think you're great, kid. Sometimes it's too hard to
be the grown up in the room, isn't it?

I need that, on more days than I can admit. I needed
encouragement so badly for one moment today I almost
face-planted in the leftover chocolate pie. But the pie won't
fill me; and somebody's words or arms or approval will fade
in a moment. It's in my Father's cover that I find true refuge
. . . even if it is from my own silly, insecure, love-needy
heart.

Father, we give you this day. It's hard out there, and the

15

demands don't seem to end. As deadlines loom and our to-dos grow, help us to run to your shelter every time we feel less-than. Help us to venture out in the world clothed in your promises and warmed by your love. Amen.

Rest deep, friend, and hide beneath His wings.

7.

Spa Day

Don't you know that your body is a sanctuary of the Holy Spirit who is in you, whom you have from God? You are not your own, for you were bought at a price. Therefore glorify God in your body.
1 Corinthians 6:19-20

We drove past the oceanfront spa at least fifty times, and every time Jack suggested I should go. Everyone said they gave the best massages. I would shake my head, shake it off, stare out the window, and change the subject. I never went, even though I love massages, even though I often need a good massage. Year after year we go to Oma Janie's cabin right down the street from the beautiful spa. I thought about making an appointment, Jack would suggest that I make an appointment, but I never even considered going.

I struggle with self-care. Mustering up the energy to make an appointment to do something relaxing seems like so much work. And I struggle with spending money on myself for something so intangible. I struggle with doing nice things for myself at all. I already feel entangled in a web of dates and times, between therapists and psychiatrists, chiropractors and dentists, notwithstanding all of the kids' appointments. Adding in more scheduled time slots on vacation seems a ridiculous joke when all I'm trying to do is escape my overly scheduled schedule. But this year, I reconsidered the beautiful oceanfront spa. This year, I finally made an appointment.

This year, I sat in the hearth room snuggled in a fluffy white bathrobe while I waited for my massage in front of a huge fireplace. I stared over the roaring fire through the floor to ceiling windows at the breathtaking view of the shining bay and the sea birds coasting on the winds. The view mesmerized me so completely I couldn't focus on the book I held in my hands. I could have stayed in the hearth room forever, but my masseuse finally called my name.

After my luxurious massage, I soaked in a shell-lined pool and stared again out at the bay. The only thing I could think while absorbing the beauty and care into my body and soul was "thank you." *Thank you that I have this opportunity to be in this beautiful place on this earth in this beautiful spa. Thank you that we can pay for this. But thank you the very most that something deep inside of me has healed enough that I can allow myself to have this beautiful experience, Lord. Thank you so much for this healing.*

I sat there in that pool and wondered what inside of me had changed. Why had it taken so long for me to receive this beautiful gift? Why, for so long, could I not come to this place? Why could I not treat my body and myself well? I think the more I have taken time to treat myself well, the more I have done to fill my basic needs, the easier it has become to believe I deserve to come to a place like this. I think for so long I was used to going without and feeling bad about myself. In some deep place inside myself, I believed that is what I deserved. But not anymore. Now I know I deserve to treat myself and love my body well.

I left the spa that day after I had taken every shower, used every product, squeezed every lotion.

I whispered thank you, thank you, thank you, all the way to my car. And I drove home full.

Is there something tugging at your heart today, friend? Is there an appointment you need to make? Maybe it's not a massage, but maybe there is something you need to do to take care of yourself? I know how difficult it can be to take the time to care for yourself, but you know that you are worth it. So go on. Take the time. Pick up the phone.

Schedule the appointment. And go. You are worth the time, the effort, and the money. You deserve to feel nurtured and loved and filled to the brim, too.

Lord, Thank you for this body that works so well. Thank you that I can still enjoy life with this body, that I can still taste and see and feel your goodness. Thank you for continuing to teach me how to care for myself, to accept that I need to love and nurture and care for myself, and that You love to see me care for myself. You say that I am "very good", that my body is "very good", and that caring for myself is "very good." Thank you for making me "very good." Amen.
(from Genesis 1:31)

Dear Lord,
I bring You my desperate need to feel safe
in a world constantly shifting under my feet.
I ask that you will reveal to me,
as I learn to count my blessings
in good times and bad,
all the ways You have been faithful
so that I can build a rock-solid trust
to hold me fast through life's circumstances.
Help me to know deep in my bones
my security can only be found in
You,
my Rock and Redeemer.
Amen

8.
Prayer to Remember

I wrote the "Prayer to Remember" after going back through my journal entries from our time when Samuel was a newborn in the NICU at Children's Hospital. It's amazing how easily we forget how much we have, even when we have been through extraordinary circumstances. This prayer is for all of us to remember just how much we have, and how little we really actually need.

August 29, 2011
Driving in our packed Pathfinder yesterday morning, it hit me: all we needed (minus Sam) we had with us: clothes, a pack and play, car seats, a stroller. Despite missing our house and all the comforts it provides, we don't need much, especially now that all we can think about is getting Sam healthy and being able to take him home. And, it's the same for all the families here at Children's Hospital, I think . . . it doesn't matter how much money you make or how nice your house is or what you can afford when your kid is sick. In a heartbeat, we would all give everything in exchange for leaving the hospital, family in tact. Family "in tact . . ." We can get by with what's in the back seat, if only we can keep each other.

2018
Lord, I often forget about those days
when just being able to bring my family home
filled every waking thought.
Nothing else mattered to me.
I ached for a normal life of diapers and dishwashers.
Now I wonder how big I've let my life become,

how littered?
How carried away I've become that I forget
about those days spent trapped in a hospital room.
These same people,
on this journey beside me
every day,
and all I think about is the trouble they cause me:
the dirty laundry and sink full of dishes,
homework to finish
and the dinner that still needs making.
My mouth runs, Lord,
and if I just stop to hear myself—
would that woman in the hospital room even recognize
me?
The handsome man
driving alongside in this same packed car,
looks straight ahead.
I watch the way he sets his jaw
when he doesn't think I'm looking,
catching him every so often in a pause
as he carries so much more
than his share of our haul.
I wonder the last time
I stopped for a thank you—
Just stopped to say,
I couldn't carry this with anyone but you?
I turn around to those faces
morphing in the backseat,
laughing and bickering and
making gross boy noises at each other
and I marvel they're siting there at all.
That we're all here.
And I whisper thank you.
I realize in an instant

I would give it all
to keep this family
for one more day.
And I hope if she could see me
from that hospital room
somewhere down the line she'd know:
I'm doing my best to keep them.
Maybe it's messy and
maybe it's louder than we thought, I keep losing my
temper—
but we're not letting go.
Thank you for helping us keep on
keeping each other.
Amen.

9.

Prayer of Thanks for Enough

They did not thirst when he led them through the deserts; he made water flow for them from the rock; he split the rock and water gushed out.
Isaiah 48:21

When I remember to stop and count the gifts given me, I see miracles everywhere. I fall in love with every day, transfixed as I witness the mundane transform into the extraordinary. A flower becomes a blessing in the hands of a pudgy-handed toddler. A cup of coffee steaming becomes a gift when poured by a friend. That which I take for granted presents as gift. And I am reminded, again and again, that every moment provides enough.

I peer outside and love the golden leaves still clinging to trees through grey pouring days. I love the answer to a thousand prayers represented in the sound of little pj'd feet pitter-pattering down our staircase in the morning. I love cupboards overflowing with food and the energy even to ladle pancake batter onto a greasy skillet on Sunday mornings. All the good things, all the tangibles, all the smellables, tastables, huggables of life are easy for me to see and easy to say, "thank You" for.

But there are other provisions, some not so easy for me to see. At the time, I didn't think of them as provisions because I was too busy holding the ceiling up. But now I can look back on the dark days when all I could do was put one foot in front of the other.

I am starting to see now things I couldn't see then. I am starting to realize more and more that in those days of ceiling holding, breath holding, of pure grit, that the floor beneath us held firm.

Did it hold firm for you, too? And did you notice that when there were empty cupboards and drained bank accounts and broken spirits that somehow just enough showed up right when you couldn't hold anymore, right when you couldn't breathe anymore? Did you notice that? *Did that happen for you, too?* It happened for us. It just kept happening: enough. Just enough. This miracle of enough just kept breaking through, always kept coming through for us. He just kept coming through for us.

Enough isn't sexy, and it's not always even tasty. I wonder if manna was satisfying: wafer-like, with no shelf life whatsoever. But there was always enough manna for the Hebrews in the wilderness. And somehow, God's still raining down manna—He's still raining down enough—on His people.

He is raining down ENOUGH for you today. I challenge you, my friend, to look into your life with "enough" eyes. See where provision rains down for you to survive, where water flows from rocks and birds fall from skies. And even if it's not sexy provision, even if it's not new stuff, praise God that it's enough.

Thanks starts in the little, in the enough providing oxygen to breathe, food for today, grace to trust for tomorrow.

I was young and now I am old, yet I have never seen the
righteous forsaken or their children begging bread.
Psalm 37:25

Lord, we praise you that even if we can't feel it, even if we
feel like we are holding the ceiling up with everything we've
got, that you're holding the floor up. You're hemming us in,
you're providing what we can't even see coming. We pray

for provision. We pray for protection. We pray that you will give us wisdom and help us to have "enough" eyes and grateful hearts.
We thank you, Lord. Amen.

10.

When You're Drowning
in Laundry Or Life

May the God of hope fill you with all joy and peace as you
trust in him, so that you may overflow with hope by the
power of the Holy Spirit.
Romans 15:13

I had been folding laundry for days. We had just returned from taking the boys camping this summer, and I was exhausted. Because of the burn ban (when is the last time you remember not being able to have a campfire in Washington state? Really?), we changed reservations at the last-minute and headed down the Oregon coast. We set up and took down three campsites in a matter of eight days. Yes, you read that right.

And even though there was a burn ban on, even though I already wanted to go home early, even though the Pacific Northwest was in the middle of a drought, it rained while we were camping at the beach. Yes, in the streak of scorched earth, drought, and burn bans we Seattleites have no clue what to do with, the rain did find us at the beach.

Everything: every pillow, sleeping bag, and piece of clothing we had packed needed to be washed.

With my medium-sized washing machine, that took four days.

We did manage to have some fun. We walked with the kids as they rode their bikes, spent time at the beach, climbed trees, and went on rides. There were campfires and even some really good dinners. I came home so tired I could barely speak, and the laundry just seemed to be a dirty joke. Literally: so dirty.

27

But, last night, as the boys were moaning about carrying more clothes and pillows up the stairs, as I felt that I would drown in my family's laundry once and for all, a tiny realization caught a hold of me. I kept tearing up at this little stack of school uniforms that arrived in the mail while we were gone that I had washed clean and folded along with all of the camping clothes.

Do you know what is so amazing about this stack of uniforms?

Do you know what made my heart swell and my eyes brim?

This simple thought: *I bought these uniforms a size too big because I know Abraham will grow into them.*

As I folded that little stack of new slacks and polos, I marveled at my audacity and certainty. I marveled at my own hope. Hope from this mother whose first baby was lost because he didn't grow. This mother who crammed protein smoothies and ding-dongs down her throat (the good fats and the bad, right?) during her second pregnancy to ensure this baby would grow. This mother who pumped every bottle full of breast milk her heart baby drank, just to fill it with a serving of formula, to make sure he would grow. This mother who laced every ounce of homemade, antibiotic- and hormone-free food she fed her children with organic butter and olive oil to help them grow. This mother who sat in her car after well baby check-ups and cried year after year because her babies were always at the bottom of the growth chart, no matter how she tried to make them grow.

Now, that mother buys clothes a half-size up because she's sure they'll grow. Now, that mother swims in laundry and Legos and teaches little boys how to fold laundry and put it away. That monstrous fear, that nagging itch at the back of her heart has slowly given way to certain hope. Where did that hope come from, Lord? That certainty that used to be so fear-haunted, so timid, so human and frail?

I am beginning to understand Paul's words in Romans 5:3-5:

We know that suffering produces perseverance; perseverance, character; and character, hope. And hope does not put us to shame, because God's love has been poured out into our hearts through the Holy Spirit, who has been given to us.

God's love has been poured out into our hearts. His love. And through our struggles, our dark days when we don't possibly see how olive oil-infused, homemade, organic food can be any kind of weapon against our deepest, darkest fears, we persevere.

Whatever little perseverance you can manage to drum up today, He will use it.

And He will pour, pour, pour more into you.

Friends, we are all scarred by life's heart breaks. We all have wounds that masquerade as fears.

Here is the truth you can take home today:

Hope can be born in the midst of this very moment's struggle. In Him, through Him, your suffering can be transformed and become perseverance and become character and become hope.

What hopeful act can you muster today in the face of your fears?

How can the Holy Spirit pour into you today?

What is the fear, pain, or struggle tripping you up today that will be your stack of laundry, your audacious hope tomorrow?

Thank you, Lord, for promising that you will turn my everyday perseverance into hope. Give me the strength to keep trying, keep pressing on when I am afraid, when I am struggling. Help me to feel you near me when I don't know

what to do next. Help me to feel your hope in small things,
Lord. Amen.

11.
Rest Upon His shore

Deep calls to deep at the thunder of your cataracts; all your
waves and your billows have gone over me. By day the Lord
commands his steadfast love, and at night his song is with
me, a prayer to the God of my life.
Psalm 42:7-8

I must confess: I'm tired, a bit worn thin. I'm burned
out, honestly. I've been feeling so ambivalent about reading
my Bible or doing devotions or writing or even going to
church. And so, I've been taking a break. And I was feeling
so badly about it, so guilty. But Psalm 42 keeps speaking to
me.

I have braved the waves for months now: paddling with
all of my strength, swimming against God and giving way to
His waves and billows again and again. I have listened and
drunk deeply the seawaters of change and I have finally,
finally washed up upon the shores. All I have been doing is
stretching, and changing, and coming up for air. For months.
I am exhausted, and it is time to take a rest.

And I balk at myself for trying to catch my breath.
He whispers soft to me,

I am the God of the billows and the shore. I am the
maker of the tide you swim in, as well as the rhythms of your
own body and the seasons of this earth. Just because you
change position does not mean you are not still beholden to
these rhythms.

Just because I sit, long enough to catch my breath and
dry in the sun does not mean I am not where I'm supposed
to be. He did not mean for every night to be a wrestling
match. Nor does every walk upon the beach require a near-

drowning exercise in change. Sometimes the beach just wants to be strolled. He wants us to rest as much as he wants us to strive.

We get so wrapped up in this culture of doing that we forget God commanded us to rest one out of every seven days. If we need to miss a Sunday of church, if we need to take some time out from community to rest, then we need to take the time. Rest your body, friend. Rest your mind and your heart. Curl up with your family by the fire, eat pancakes in your pajamas, and rest. Or stay in bed with a good book and let your partner take your kids to church. I am amazed at what a day of going nowhere can accomplish when I am exhausted.

So if you are feeling tired like I am, rest, friend. When it's time to wrestle the waves again, you'll know. Believe in the God who made everything within and outside of you to be seasonal. Day and night, tides and seasons: we are made to turn over with this world, working and stretching and birthing fruit. Then, we are made perfectly to rest.

Obey His command to rest. Sink into it, like the wet sand on the edge of the water's lap. Sink into an idea of God that grows bigger than your understanding, bigger than any one thing you could ever accomplish for Him. Trust Him that He is working it all out for your good.

And rest. I'm trying to, right along with you.

Lord, we pray that you will still our hearts to rest in you. We know that you have made us to rest as much as you have made us to strive. Please fill our hearts with peace. Amen.

12.
He is Our Hiding Place

Therefore let all who are faithful offer prayer to you; at a time of distress, the rush of mighty waters shall not reach them. You are a hiding place for me; you preserve me from trouble; you surround me with glad cries of deliverance.
Selah
Psalm 32:6-7

Do you feel like me today, like if you stop for one second this list of tasks and appointments will rush right over you? Let's take a moment to breathe and remember:

He Is Our Hiding Place

from the screaming two year old and the colicky baby and the grade schooler who forgot to inform you about the science project that is due TODAY, from the piles of laundry and bills and worries. He is our Hiding Place. And in the midst of the chaos, He preserves us. He surrounds us. He shouts out to us, over every inch of our distress. He shouts out over the waters that we are His, that we are spoken for.

Yahweh your God is among you,
a warrior who saves.
He will rejoice over you with gladness.
He will bring you quietness with His love.
He will delight in you with shouts of joy.
Zephaniah 3:17

Lord, help us to find You today. Help us to hide in You. Teach us Your cries of deliverance, Your victory songs. Amen.

13.
I See The Roses

See! The winter is past; the rains are over and gone.
Flowers appear on the earth; the season of singing has
come . . .
Song of Songs 2:11-12

Our front porch is one of my favorite places in the world. Living in Seattle in a constant state of downpour, it is the one place we can stand outside without getting wet. When our house rocks with family parties, guests spill out onto the front porch for fresh air, someone always finding their way to the swinging conversation bench at the end of the porch. Fuchsias spill out of the window boxes, and flowers reach through the spindles of the railing, as if to join in on the fun.

Today, however, is not the porch's finest hour. Due to an overly busy spring, I forgot to tend the flowerbeds and water the flower boxes. Flowers died.

I'm pausing for a moment out of respect and guilt.

Stinging nettles settled in, which has never, ever happened on my watch before. Clover invaded. I will not even write the details of the rose garden mess in the backyard . . .

In my attempts to rehabilitate the front garden, I have spent my spare time pulling weeds and replanting. Unfortunately, this process has proven slow and messy.

It's not pretty, even overwhelming. It was even a little embarrassing this week when friends came for dinner. I winced as I warned them not to trip on the garden hose.

I could focus on the mess and the wince and be terribly discouraged, but that's not the view I choose to see.

35

What I choose to see instead is the little pink fairy rose climbing through the porch swing. I choose to focus on that. It's quite a miracle, actually. That rose started growing all on its own on the edge of our property, an offshoot of my neighbor lady's beautiful bush. Last spring, I transplanted two tiny little rose stems from the edge of our property into my flowerbeds. I had no idea if they'd survive, let alone flourish. One year later, these two tiny little stems have blossomed into bushes, climbing and blooming into pink fairy heaven. And all I did was dig them up and plant them in good soil.

The roses peek through the bench and climb the chimney and remind me that not everything in this life is hard. Sometimes the flowers just show up, pink and scenty, with enough fragrance to make me forget the mess.

I count these roses for the gifts they are, and am reminded of other gifts making me giggle: tiny hot pink English daisies I planted years ago still manage to pop up every spring with their yellow bellies shining proudly, Violas reseeding and reproducing in weed-like fashion, their dark violet petals arranged to look like faces popping up throughout my garden, and the darling brown rabbit (Sam named him "Carrots") who occasionally hops onto our porch to say hello before bounding away into my messy gardens. He seems to enjoy them as much as I do.

With my coffee in hand, while the kids still sleep, I pen thanks for these gifts I didn't earn, these reminders of a God who took the time to paint faces on a pansy, these constant promises of renewal and constancy and cotton tails.

We sit at our dining room table and open the window over the overgrown rose garden, marveling that even though I neglected them, despite the fact they grow amongst the weeds and didn't get fertilized or trimmed, they bloom.

Even as my guilt and nag self-deprecate me with

shoulds and comparisons to other women who actually tend their roses, His voice sways through tree branches,

Drink them in, marvel. Hold petals, feel their silk between your fingers. Gawk at a beauty that will outlive all of your failures. Know I breathe even into these just for your delight.

I whisper thank you, and choose to see this view. I see the roses.
What view will you choose to see today?

Lord, please help me to see the roses today. Please help me to see past the messes to see what you view as beautiful. Help me not to get so caught up in the mundane in life that I forget to say thank you. Amen.

14.
The View From Here

Enter into His gates with thanksgiving,
And into His courts with praise.
Be thankful to Him, and bless His name.
For the Lord is good;
His mercy is everlasting,
And His truth endures to all generations.
Psalms 100:4-5

Gratitude was not one of the emotions filling my heart after ten days in the NICU with my newborn heart baby, Samuel. I asked his nurse how long she thought it would take for us to leave the hospital with him.

"Oh, by Christmas for sure."

I almost fainted, and a pulse of strangle-you anger rushed through my exhausted body. "Christmas? It's August!"

"You just never know how these things are going to go--"

I looked at her and tried not to reveal the churning of my heart, the fear that I didn't have what it took to stay until Christmas. I ached for our older son, now living at my parents for the second week in a row. He didn't understand where we had gone; only two years old, he struggled with such swift changes to his daily life. The parents who carried him down the stairs every morning, played with, fed and loved him every day, had all but vanished.

I felt a wave of homesickness flood over me. I could almost feel the warm air wafting through the sliding door in the kitchen, the curtains dancing in the breeze, filtering in the late summer afternoon's rays. I longed for the lush grass in our mess of a back yard, to lie down and savor it like I had never taken the time to do before now. I dreamed of a home free of wires and alarms going off constantly, where I could hold both of my living babies in my arms. I wondered if we would ever leave this place, if we would ever place this baby in the crib his big brother had slept in, ever see him grow.

And then, just days later, we did take him home. I held both of my babies on my lap and cried tears of relief and joy. We placed Samuel in the crib his big brother slept in as a newborn. We have watched him grow against all odds, and we have marveled.

Gratitude has assumed a new form. What I used to take for granted, I now say thank you for. When I was pregnant with Samuel and completely overwhelmed, filled with anxiety at the thought of driving to the hospital for yet another check up, I started thanking God for concrete. Yup. You see, I started thinking about those mamas in Africa whose babies were sick like mine. But there are no concrete roads and SUVS to get them to the hospital, if there is a hospital at all for them to go to. They walk barefoot in sweltering heat while I drive in air conditioning.

I started giving thanks for the freedom to choose which doctors treated me and Sam, as well as which hospital he would go to. And for nurses. And ultra sound machines. And health insurance. And the nice old millionaire who dies and leaves money for families who have health insurance and jobs and have saved their money, but never enough money to cover seventeen days in the NICU. And Aunt Mary, and all the people who had been there before us sleeping on the floor or leaving their babies because there was no room for parents to sleep in the ICU. Because of our Aunt Mary Schwed, who spent two thirds of our cousin Matthew's life at Children's Hospital, and parents like her, we slept in a bed in a private room a floor away from

Samuel, took free, clean showers and washed our clothes in a free laundry room with free detergent. Because she suffered, we gained. Because she wanted more for those families coming after her, we slept in peace. Thank you.

My heart has not stopped this swelling of gratitude. Yes, I have struggled and pulled inward at times. I have been too tired to give thanks, too tired to lift my head up. But, now, even when I'm cowering and chewing on my self-pity, I am staring at concrete. And then I am thankful again.

I would never choose the life I live for anyone else, but I wish, *oh how I wish*, that you could see the view from here. From here, God is a God of mothers' pounding hearts, of dirt roads, and air-conditioned ultra sound rooms. He stretches and bears me up in a deep ocean of love as I wait for Him on desperate knees. In my suffering, in my losing, in my mourning, and in my bearing, I see more of Him in every breath, in every cup of coffee and echocardiogram. I see more from here. And I sing thanks.

Praise be to the God tending sick babies, praise be to the God who walks with their mamas and papas. Praise be to the God who walks with all of us in our struggles, who never leaves us no matter how lost we may feel in our fight. May you feel him in your desperate moments, Mama. May you learn to see God working in each of your thanksgivings. May you know how He loves you and each of your babies so desperately, so personally. May you count it all the way up into a love so big it can only equal Him.

Lord, help me never forget the view of gratitude. Help me never forget all the ways that you have provided for me, even when things are hard. I pray that you will give me a grateful heart in all circumstances so that I praise you always. Amen.

15.
What No One Tells You At Your Baby Shower

Surely there is a future, and your hope will not be cut off.
Proverbs 23:18

It's been a long time since I was my own, since I wasn't wrapping myself around the dreams and needs of another. But it was long before my wedding day that this wrapping began. I gave so easily to love, pliable and self-sacrificing in my youth. I gave without counting, as if there would be no cost. But wrapping meant unwrapping all of me, phasing from daughter and child to woman and wife. I relinquished one identity, one head of household, and embraced all that my new name represented, all that would now be expected. I phased out of the old way, identity, roles.

My life has become a set of phases: daughter to wife, sick to healthy, pregnant to bereaved, bereaved mother of a rainbow baby, pregnant with a terminal baby, NICU mom, heart mom, half-time mom to a kindergartener and a preschooler, and now before- and after-school mom.

That list of words looks ridiculously trite: a litany of simple nouns and adjectives. But every word of every line completely transformed my life. Every word represents hours and weeks and years of changing: my constant, rapid shedding of one way and blind, deliberate running–naked and vulnerable–into a new form of myself. Every word required a new struggle, a new prayer, a new rhythm.

Every new phase felt like it would go on forever. The long nights would never end; the worry would never cease. And then, the finale of it all slipped by me in a blink.

After changing the boys' diapers, one after the other for four solid years, our Samuel potty-trained himself completely in one day. Box of diapers sat, collecting dust, in the corner of his room. We tucked brothers into bunk beds and packed the crib away. They giggled in delight as they snuggled into their brothers' room, and we marveled at their little forms fast asleep in such big beds. Just like that, the baby phase ended.

I told everyone how excited I felt to be finished with the baby phase. Still, every so often when I stood in the garage, nose in the freezer, I turned to see the skeleton of their crib waiting for a more permanent spot in the attic. As a familiar longing for just one more baby would rise up in my throat, I recalled all of the late night, tearful talks with Jack and all the reasons why Samuel is our last. My eyes filled; the baby phase really was finished.

My heart swelled with sadness, wondering how I would survive all of these phases, this battered mother's heart that loves to bruising. I gasped at the length of these hard years of lugging and planning around naps and freezing and defrosting baggies of breast milk. Suddenly, my babies walked on their own insistence and ate with forks and told me when they needed to go to the potty. I was left speechless.

Breathe in, breathe out. And the phasing turns again.

The next phase: a school full of strangers, and when do I drop off a kindergartener when school starts at 8:45? And is my three-year-old in too much preschool or not enough? And how is it that as they begin new phases of their lives, so must I? How do I become room-mom and field-trip-mom and make-t-shirts-for-the-100th-day-of-school-mom? They did not cover those topics in college. This is what they don't tell you when you're swollen and eating cake at your baby shower: the phasing doesn't end. We as mothers forever change, adapt, fix our schedules as our children change. What they need, we become. Does this humble anyone else? Is it a bit difficult to swallow this truth? It comes to me in waves, this phasing. It comes to me high in the chest, like panic. I used to wake in the middle of the night panicked over Samuel starting preschool. This is not the midnight panic as we waited for his open-heart surgery, or the next doctor's appointment. I had to remind myself: this is normal mom panic. I should be getting used to this panic: the tidal in and out of phasing. I should be getting used to this drop in my gut, the same as the big down on a rollercoaster ride.

And now, I drop them off at the front doors of their elementary school. I drive away, with an entire day to fill without them. Without them? How is there life without them, when my whole life has been dancing around them these past years? How do I shrink back down into myself, when I have spent the last years growing around them?

Truth is, I don't think I can shrink. I think I'm forever stretched, always reaching . . . phasing. Loving these men of mine into manhood, into death and life and out of hospitals and cribs and into schools has phased me in and out of identities and body sizes and sleep schedules and hormone levels. Loving these men of mine continues to require my own adaptation each time they transform. And it is humbling to admit today that I am defined by their journeys, that my life is framed by who they are.

My family was my choice so long ago, and it is still my choice today. Even if there is less for me, even if it means I must now unpack this phase of swaddles and lullabies, wipe away tears after I've walked them up to their classrooms, and find a way to fill my days after they leave them so empty. And even as I sit in an empty car and grieve the end of this me, this identity, I have lived enough phases to know

there will be newfound joy in the next.
So I breathe in, and I breathe out. And I wait for the new phase to begin.

There are far, far better things ahead than anything we leave behind. -Cs Lewis

Lord, please help me in this stretching as my children grow and change. I continue to grow and change, too, Lord, and now I'm wondering what to do with all of these feelings. Where do I fit in all of this? No one ever asks me how I feel when they suddenly grow out of a phase. Lord, could you tend to my heart? Could you sit with me a while? I could use some tending as I grieve this phase before I move on to the next one. Amen.

Bless you in your phasing, Mama.

16.

Twisted Bliss

You have turned my mourning into dancing; you have taken
my sackcloth and clothed me with joy, so that my soul may
praise you and not be silent. O LORD my God, I will give
thanks to you forever.
Psalm 30:11-12

Thank God for children and flowers. I don't mean
"thank God," like "thank God" the roast wasn't over cooked
or "thank God" the blueberry stains came out of another tiny
shirt. I mean, "Thank God," fall down on my knees and
raise my hands to the sky, "Thank God for children and
flowers."

Every spring since we buried Caleb, I am amazed anew
at the persistence of nature. Even as we still feel winter's
chill in March and April mornings, the fibers of life refuse
to yield, no matter the harshness of our winters or the
darkness of night. They pop up undeniable shoots of color,
demanding attention in the pouring down rain.

March brings fully round the deepest grief of my life; it
also brings forth bulbs popping, green shooting. It was on a
Wednesday of Holy week that I brought my first-born son
into the world, only to bathe him and baptize him and wrap
him in burial clothes. But it was also a Wednesday in Holy
week when I take my little gaggle to the park to meet dear
friends as we chat and drink coffee, chase after stray
ducklings, kiss war wounds, and convince the three-year
olds one rock per visit is enough to take home.

For several months now, I have been low: heavy,
gaping, with little relief . . . it's not something I can take
more meds for. Believe me; I've had that conversation with

my doctor. He asks me one question: "Is there joy in your life every day?"

I smile at him as I sit on the leather chair in his office and ponder the twisted bliss of my every day. My mind floods with story times in the pirate tent, falling asleep at nap time with a teething miracle child nuzzled into my arms, peeling apples for a crisp at the kid's table and being told, "Good job, Mom! You're a good cooker." I think of walking down the beach in ten-foot increments, stopping at Bram's insistence to help dig up plastic shovel after plastic shovel of sand. I think of how all of my "shoesies" are disappearing and reappearing throughout the house, separated and stowed away by a toddling shoe thief. I remember Bram "helping" me weed in the garden, only to realize that he was weeding out the ground cover. It's a good thing creeping Jenny creeps quickly!

I smile back at my doctor, at his kind eyes: "There is joy in every moment."

I used to think that I could separate my life into strands, unraveling the sad from the happy, and the grief from the joy. The older I become, however, the more I realize that grief begets joy if we allow its soul-carving to be filled with the Holy Spirit. What is lost gives birth to new eyes of gratitude: what I used to pass over, now I stop, kneel, and give thanks for.

I recently read Ann Voskamp's *One Thousand Gifts*. She proposes that life is one big gift: all the moments of happiness and sadness, fullness and emptiness. The joy of God fills these moments when we learn to stop and give thanks in all of it, for all of it. I have known this, but I forget it . . . like Peter walking on water for a moment, I lose my focus on Jesus and sink, sink, sink. But I am re-identifying myself with gratitude, resolving again to grab hold of everyday thankfulness.

So, this spring, as I do every spring, you will find me in the yard digging up dandelions and cursing at slugs. I will take multiple breaks to play swords or push a swing, rescue some little person from danger or kiss an owie. I will give thanks for the friend who brought me a pallet of hot pink tulips, only half of which I had time to plant. I will give thanks for the tulips, hot pink lipstick to the burgeoning face of our front yard, and marvel at how each flower twists and contorts to ensure its needs are met. I will scold the toddler who decapitates my precious hot-pink gifts with his chubby little hands, and then scoop him in my arms and thank God he is well enough–alive enough–to assault tulips and throw himself on the ground in a tantrum when I won't allow him to execute all of my flowers.

I think that if I am to be who God intended me to be, I must somehow learn to hold both the grief and the joy, not denying one or the other. I must somehow give thanks in all things, and search for God in the midst of my every day. He is here, sitting on the couch with me as I write this and fend off chubby fingers who threaten to delete my work in every moment. He is here when I grieve. He fills it all with a glory I cannot conjure or even imagine. He fills it all, and then calls it good. May you see the twisted bliss of your every day.

Lord, please give me eyes to see the gifts you give me. Give me a spirit to receive what is right in front of me.
Amen.

Dear Lord,
I bring You my need for relationship.
Before I go anywhere to fill myself up,
to feel understood,
approved of,
liked,
or friended,
I come to You.
I know You are the only One
who can truly fill me,
Lord Jesus.
I give you my heart.
Amen

17.
God Alone

"For God alone my soul waits in silence;
for my hope is from him."
Psalm 62:5

Next to the above verse in my Bible, the words, "Expectation in Hebrew" are scrawled out, and the word hope is circled. A line is drawn from hope to expectation. Expectation.

The word "hope" means "expectation" in Hebrew.

The NIV translates it a little differently: "My expectation comes from Him."

My hope, my expectation is from Him?

Shouldn't it be "my expectation is in Him"?

It's early morning, I'm drinking my coffee and shaking my head.

I have a problem with expectation. I put expectations in people who cannot meet them, people who cannot meet them because they are not God. Because of this, I am constantly disappointed. Then, I'm praying the same prayer: *Lord, please fill my disappointment. Please help me to look to You instead of them.*

But this morning as I read Psalm 62 alongside Beth Moore's beautiful commentary on it in *Whispers of Hope: 10 Weeks of Devotional Prayer*, I stick on this idea that God built this expectation into me. It's supposed to be there: this hole of expectation. And I am supposed to be desperate to fill it.

I just have to fill this hole with the right thing, instead of all of these other things that won't satisfy. But I keep trying to fill my space with all of the wrong things, like feeding my physical hunger with motor oil or stuffing

49

cheeseburgers into our SUV's gas tank. If I do that, I'll make myself sick, and the car will not run.

I will never be fully satisfied until I turn to God to fill this expectation. He designed me with an appetite for Him alone.

Beth Moore explained it so well that whispering the two words, "God Alone," to yourself when someone disappoints you can change everything. God Alone. God Alone.

I think about all the times I pin my expectations on another person, *if only they will do this one thing for me. If only they will be this one thing for me. If only they will show up for me.* And when they don't, I am crushed. I get so hopping mad. I can't forgive. But why? Because if it was God alone I needed to be the one thing for me, show up for me, come through for me, would I be so upset with people when they get it wrong?

If God alone, then I fill up long before I turn to people for relationship. When I turn to people once my pitcher is filled with God alone, once my need for approval and love is met, once I'm satiated, my relationships look different. They no longer serve to primarily fill me up, but rather to be places of communion. I walk into relationships already overflowing, which is a good deal different than walking in palms out-stretched, desperate, and needing.

When I depend on God Alone, my pitcher overflows. When I practice the pitcher life and go to God first to meet my safety and relationship needs, my heart is full before I approach my loved ones.

Practice saying it with me: "God Alone."

No one else, nothing else, will fill me. Nothing else will satisfy.

So, Lord: please fill me. Please teach me to turn toward you when I need, when I hunger, when I'm expecting. Please teach me to whisper, "GOD ALONE," and live a life of dependence based solely on these words. God Alone. Amen.

18.
Prayer for a Friend

Lord,
As I hold these little hands
and bravely come into this new place
You and I both know the new-friend prayers
I've prayed for each of them.
I let go of one hand
and then the other.
I wave good-bye
and pray,
Lord, let them make a new friend
Just one so they won't be alone in line
At recess
Or the lunch table.
But as I turn to leave, Lord,
I feel you catch my eye
and look deep in my heart.
I know You know me.
I know You know every prayer unspoken.
And yet, I leave so much unsaid.
Why is it so difficult to ask for myself?
I look around this room and wonder,
Could there be a friend for me?
A fellow mama who understands?
Who could be gentle enough with my anxious heart?
I trust you, Lord, to provide a friend for me
even though I don't trust as easily as I used to. Amen.

19.
Glory of Friendship

Now the Lord is the Spirit, and where the Spirit of the Lord is, there is freedom. And all of us, with unveiled faces, seeing the glory of the Lord as though reflected in a mirror, are being transformed into the same image from one degree of glory to another; for this comes from the Lord, the Spirit.
2 Corinthians 3:17-18

From my table in Starbucks this morning, I can see the parking lot bathed in morning light, the trees drenched in multi-colored glory, just how it used to look when Leah and I would be finishing our morning walk, and the sun would transform the darkness into pink "Dumbo" clouds. I thank God for this friendship blossomed out of our two little boys sharing a pre-kindergarten class together.

My heart was so battered from a friendship gone wrong that when Leah and her husband took the pastorship at the school's church I could barely lift my head up on the first day of school. She immediately wanted to be my friend, and I immediately wanted no part in any friendship at all. But she persisted. Persistently. It didn't help that her little boy's name happened to be Isaac. And he wanted to play with Abraham? And it wasn't a coincidence that I have a slight infatuation with the Hebrew Scriptures and might think their patriarchal names might be a sign from God?

Slowly, carefully, Leah worked her magic on me. Leah possesses friendship magic. And pretty soon, the sun rose one morning and we walked out of the darkness and watched as pink Dumbo clouds lit up the sky. And I was struck at how God had given me this beautiful friendship, even when my heart had been broken and I didn't think I could be open to friendship again. Sometimes the greatest

53

glories come out of our darkest places.

The best friendships are the ones that light up our lives with glory, the ones who meet us where we are in the darkness and accept what they find there. That's what Leah always does for me. She never tries to remake me or force me into a mold. We are different people; we have different paths. But she's always working her friendship magic, always loving, always bringing just a little bit of glory with her. Being loved by Leah is being accepted as I am. Whether I'm up on stage teaching about mental illness, or whether I've gained thirty pounds and am home-bound on antipsychotics, Leah treats me the same.

Not all of my friends have treated me the same. In fact, I have experienced quite a bit of heart break. So when I find a friend like Leah who will stick it out, who can hang with the highs and the lows? Well, I think there's glory in that.

King David found a friend like that. His name was Jonathan. Jonathan was David's friend when David was popular, and Jonathan was loyal when David was running for his life. Jonathan told his friend,

"Go in peace, for we have sworn friendship with each other in the name of the Lord, saying, 'The Lord is witness between you and me, and between your descendants and my descendants forever'"
(1 Samuel 20:42).

I don't know about you, but I want those kinds of friendships: the kind that perseveres past circumstance, that sees past the day-to-day grime. These bonds that choose each other not because of a family obligation or work relationship but because of something deeper and maybe even more true: because "we have sworn friendship." Knowing there are people out there in the world that swear friendship to me, that choose me, like Leah, can fill my heart up to overflowing on a hard day.

The greatest glory is to be that friend, like Leah, to someone else. Right where you are, there is another mom with a broken heart. Maybe she's new to the school and shy or just pushed to the max and doesn't think she has time for a friend. But you could be the Leah who bridges the gap. You could be the friend who gives the gentle nudge and encourages her to open her heart. And who knows? She might just be your friend for life.

The glory found in long-lasting friendship spills over into the world around us. The glory fills and covers us if we let it. If you look closely, you can see it in the way the morning sun lights up your morning drive. You can feel it in the way you hold your children close. Glory paints our lives, reflecting God Himself when we look straight into it.

Lord, teach me to see You in the way I love others. Teach me to see the women around me and to recognize where I can be a friend. Teach me to look straight into this moment, so that I can keep growing in Your glory and my understanding of You.
Amen.

20.
Friends in Love

Arise, come, my darling;
my beautiful one, come with me.
Song of Songs 2:13

The minute I looked at Jack I knew that he was the one for me. But, he took a while to arrive at the same revelation. While I waited patiently for him to fall madly in love with me, I endeavored to be his new best friend, to discover all the things he cared about. I watched sports with him, listened to his weird music and pretended to like it, encouraged him with notes and hugs and smiles, crafted him homemade presents and baked goods. Okay: so it is was probably pretty obvious that I was crazy about him.

Fast-forward nineteen years later to just another afternoon of us sitting in the car together. I watched as he plugged his phone into the stereo. A song came on that I hadn't heard before, and I grabbed the phone to see the title and the artist. I had never heard of the band playing through our car speakers. As I scrolled through his music library, I realized I didn't know half of the songs in his phone.

"Oh, you wouldn't like any of this," he shrugged and grabbed his phone back to change the song.

Just then, something pricked me from the inside, and I turned to him: "But if you like it, I'd still like to hear it."

He gave me a sideways glance like he didn't believe me. I couldn't remember the last time I had listened to his music. When did I stop listening to his music?

Yes, I am a loving wife. Yes, I am engaged in my marriage. But where was that young girl who just loved to be his friend, who thrilled at just hearing about his life, his struggles, and listening to his weird music?

This music thing had me bugged. I realized that it wasn't just the music that had faded into the background. I tried to remember what we used to do for fun together. I realized that, somewhere along the way, we stopped playing games. We used to play cards endlessly. I cheated at every game because he beat me no matter what I did; he pretended to be mortified by my lack of morality on the Monopoly and Canasta front. We'd laugh. A lot.

Somewhere in this roaring river of life, we stopped playing games.

And sports games? Well, let's just say I'd gotten to the point where every time he watched a game, I went up stairs and took a nap. Now to be fair: this was usually on the weekends when the kids were taking their naps. And, I was sleep-deprived for years.

But one afternoon as I was climbing the stairs to take my Sunday nap, I had a thought: this game really matters to him, and he's down there watching it by himself. If all I do is curl up next to him instead of going upstairs, at least he's not watching his game alone.

One Friday afternoon, I sat downstairs on the couch writing. The house was quiet for once, and I was actually making headway on my next blog post. I paused for a moment, as I often do, to listen for Jack. I could hear him typing in his office, and something pricked me again. It seemed so odd that we were in a house all by ourselves for an entire day and both working so hard that we hardly took time to exchange pleasantries.

Sure: we both have obligations and responsibilities. We both need to do our jobs. But, in a life where date nights are expensive and rare, what harm would there be in a day-date? Even a date lunch? Even a lunch sitting at the kitchen counter talking, our elbows sticking in the kids' syrup left over from breakfast?

I tried to remember the last movie we went to in the middle of the day. It was five and half years ago when I was pregnant with Abraham. And now? We have one afternoon a week to ourselves: to work more, of course. But, I asked myself, why? Why not work harder the rest of the week and go to a movie with my hubs on our free day instead?

I put my laptop down and raced up the stairs, barging into his office.

"Wanna go get a burrito and see a movie?" I asked him.

He turned around in his chair and stared at me in disbelief, like a child let loose in a candy store with a wad full of cash to spend.

We did escape from our responsibilities in the middle of the day: my best friend and I. It felt young and free and giddy, like we were getting away with something, like we could finally be us again, the way we used to be. We watched a movie filled with Jack humor, and I laughed at him laughing so hard at an oversized raccoon and a talking tree posing as superheroes.

We reluctantly returned home in time to get the kids: back to deadlines and time sheets and "If you don't eat five more bites of dinner–" But, our three hour field trip kept us both smiling at each other all weekend.

So grab that partner of yours and find a way to be their friend again. Whether it's watching a football game in the family room or going to a superhero movie, having fun together just being friends can do any a marriage a world of good.

Lord, I pray you will awaken that spirit inside of me that once wanted to be my husband's best friend, interested in what he cared about and wanting to be a part of his life. Please revive in me a desire to share fun things with him

again, not just as husband and wife but also as friends.
Amen

21.
To Love Again

Lord,
Midnight crawls through the dark
as I lie awake so close to this person
unearthed by the vast cavern between us.
How do love and fury ignite in an instant?
I see now Your guiding hand
molding our two hearts into better souls.
The gift this struggle births
When two hearts break upon each other day after day
When two wills keep choosing each other to the
breaking.
You knew we would hurt each other.
You knew our darkness.
You know how to turn it altogether for our good.
Marriage burns through the vanities of a spirit,
sifting through to our best form,
leaving us real, raw, open to glory.
I see You working, Lord,
even if it smacks of hurt.
I lie here and listen to my love's breathing,
And I praise You for one more day
To love again.
Amen.

22.
Why Every Marriage Needs Date Night

Above all, love each other deeply, because love covers over
a multitude of sins.
1 Peter 4:8

One Saturday during the baby years, Jack and I woke
up and cheerfully drank our coffee, discussing all we
planned to accomplish throughout our day. We avoided any
and all disagreements because we set our sights on what
really mattered: tonight was date night. To have a sitter, the
money to actually go out on a date, and the time to do so
rarely happened then. We agreed on a plan to divide and
conquer our chores and set out to do so. Or, so we thought.

That afternoon, I returned from the grocery store with
high hopes and shiny toes still glossy from my pedicure, and
my arms full of groceries, with a good forty-five minutes
left to primp for our date. But my happy-hearted date night
high tanked as I surveyed the state of our home. Somewhere
in my girly imagination I envisioned returning from errand
running to a clean house. At least, I imagined that the floors
would be gleaming and the kitchen counters would be
crumb-free.

As I walked over crunchy floors to set the groceries on
the cluttered dining room table, I surveyed a downstairs
littered with dirty dishes, toys and laundry strewn
everywhere. I walked in circles, frozen, as a tidal wave of
frustration swept me up in a flood of self-pity and
hopelessness: *Life is too hard. There is never enough time.*
What's the point of going out on a date when there is so
much work yet to do? Couldn't he do more while the kids
were awake? Why does he always have work to do when I
need him to do something?

61

By the time he came downstairs, my cheeks burned red with tears and self-pity. The verdict was in: Jack didn't care one bit about my needs. He didn't care at all. His face, strangely, blanked. "Why are you crying?"

"The house! The floors! It's a mess!" I blubbered.

"So?"

"You were supposed to clean while I ran the errands-"

"Um, I told you I had work to do-"

INTERMISSION

I completely forgot Jack's mention of a "little extra work to do" during our cheerful coffee conversation that morning. In all of my excitement, I hadn't heard him. As I remembered this very important fact, I should have stopped myself. I should have said, "Oh, that's right. I forgot." But my humility had run away with any modicum of reason by that point. I already held the verdict in my hand: Jack was guilty.

END INTERMISSION.

So, there we stood in the kitchen, yelling, me crying, Jack incredulous. My unrealistic expectations cause more undue strife in my marriage than any other one issue . . . and that's saying something.

After fifteen minutes of fighting over–well, nothing, really–he looked at me, "I'm going to cancel the babysitter. This is ridiculous." He was right; it was. I was.

I grabbed his arm, right as he reached for his phone: "No, we can't. She's already given up her Saturday night. I'll just go get ready, and we can just get out of here. We can split up if you want to. We don't have to go somewhere together. We just need to get out of here for a night."

He agreed. I primped and Jack dutifully cleaned. We left an hour after the babysitter arrived.

Once in the car, I looked at my handsome husband, jaw set tight the way he does when he is so angry with me. My words cut through the dark silence: "I'm sorry. I don't know what got into me. I just didn't think you cared—"

He turned to face me as his jaw softened just a bit. We filled the car with every stress and every fear and every unmet need that builds in the niceness, in the trying, in the Saturday mornings and Tuesday nights at 3 am when the baby will not sleep. We counted up the stressors, the reasons, the sorrys and I-forgive-yous until we were back to neutral. Just talking it all out and being real about how hard every day is was exhausting enough to turn the car around and go to bed early.

We sat silent, his jaw a little more relaxed. "I think we should still go to dinner," I said, breaking the silence. "But I don't think we should go as us. Let's be another couple tonight. Let's be a couple with healthy, perfectly behaved children. Let's be a couple without a million expenses and worries. Let's be interesting. Let's small-talk politics and magazine articles; let's drink too much wine and have to sit and drink coffee to sober up. Let's be who we'd be without all the hard." I grabbed his forearm as another tear ran down my cheek. "I just want to be the old us, you know?"

He turned to see me for the first time since my kitchen explosion. "Okay, I can do that."

We went to our favorite restaurant and we sat for four hours. We laughed at each other and flirted like we were light, like the corners of our world weren't just about to tear open and gush the flood in. I forgot to see him as child care relief, as garbage take-out man, as budget keeper. I remembered how much fun he is, how we don't need entertainment when we go out because we have so much fun just talking. I remembered him: the man I love.

We drove home and paid the babysitter, all the details of our life flooding in as we walked up the stairs to bed. And it may have only been four hours, but it felt like oxygen to us, after months of holding our breath trying not to drown.

We decided date night would have to fit in the budget more regularly, because we all have to breathe sometimes.

So, go on date night anyway. We do.

Lord, please give me the wisdom to hear my partner instead of just hearing what I want to hear. Please help me to remember to say I'm sorry when I'm wrong, to make up the difference where I can, and to go on date night whenever possible.
Amen.

'

Dear Lord,
I trust you with my value,
believing when You call me "very good,"
daughter, beloved, and altogether beautiful,
that I truly am all of these things.
It's just that the minute I walk out of Your
presence,
I start to forget.
Can you help me remember,
Lord,
all day long?
When I'm doing dishes,
driving the carpool,
in the midnights and
early mornings?
Please help me remember I'm your girl.
It's easy to forget out here in this world.
Amen

23.
Abba's Girl

And I pray that you, being rooted and established in love, may have power, together with all the Lord's holy people, to grasp how wide and long and high and deep is the love of Christ . . .
Ephesians 3: 17-18

Every time I step into new, take a risk, stand up, I steal a moment when no one's looking. I hide in the bathroom and look at myself in the mirror. I stare hard, past the quick hair brush and smear-enough-plaster-to-hide-all-the-flaws weekday morning routine. I furrow my eyebrows, purse my lips, put my game face on serious.

I look hard in the mirror at the peach fuzz all over my face that magically appeared when I swelled with my first babe. *Why do I have such a hard time remembering to wax it?* I think about the arms I know need to be in shape *but aren't*. I wonder if I just get serious about a smoothie diet for two more weeks if I'll finally fit into the smaller size.

I look at my website, how the numbers still are so very small, and how my platform is more like a 2x4 I'm balancing on than a stage from which to profligate. I stare even closer in the mirror, remembering every time I've lost my temper with my boys when they're lolly-gagging over their eggs and playing monster with their clothes half over their heads instead of shipping up so we can ship out.

And I pray, "Lord, are you sure you got the right person?"

Because I'm not exactly together. You might have seen me sitting outside of Nordstrom last week, digging through a mountain of receipts.

Or maybe you saw me in Starbucks two days later

working so furiously on a book proposal that, after two hours, I realized I never ordered a drink.

Maybe you've noticed that I see my therapist regularly, because nothing helps keep bipolar 1 disorder in check like good, old-fashioned talk therapy. Or did you notice me in the Costco Pharmacy paying full tilt for my lithium because I never seem to find the time to order the 90-day supply that my insurance will actually cover.

There are pieces of my life that look like a mess. Relationships that I don't have the answers for. Brokenness I keep praying for healing over, but haven't found yet. Wounds that feel more like black holes seething through me, sucking my gravity in with them.

For years, I have looked at my life and told my Father, "This girl is not the one for public display. Look at her: everywhere You look there's a problem, an issue, a brokenness. *Look at her past, Lord!* I mean, people might understand the bipolar, but add in all the rest? This is too much, too much."

But He keeps loving me. And after several months swimming in the gospel truth of Brennan Manning's *Ragamuffin Gospel* I'm glimpsing my Abba's view of me.

she's little. A child, really. with her hair undone messy, like mine used to be in the mornings when I woke up quiet and came down the hallway in my Hello Kitty nightgown. her cheeks are chubby from gobbling that extra cupcake when Mama wasn't looking. she's smiling morning-sweet, breaking dawning, because she knows her Abba adores her. She knows.

She knows who she is: *Her Father's Daughter.*

She knows what she's worth: *His Own Son.*

She knows where she's been: *He's been with her the whole time.*

She knows where she's going: *Her Father's House.*

She knows what He wants for her: *To be wrapped up in His love, to live assured, to not fear.*

So that's what I'm doing: being His little girl, asking in my deepest, fear-filled, curled-up-in-bed afternoons, that He be my Father and Mother and break through my humanness and fill me up with Abba-love, that there be so much love in my heart that past and present doesn't matter: because *I am his.*

And when I stumble ten times a day? *I am his.*

And when I don't know what to do next? *I am His.*

When I am waiting for Him to move, wondering if I heard Him wrong? If all of this is just a little crazy?

I'm Abba's girl.

And so are you. God bless you, and may you know the reality of what it is to be Abba's girl. May the truth of His love flood your heart. May the love only the Father can give grow within you. Ask Him to show you and He will. He will show You His love. You will know this love, friend. And it will change everything.

Abba, thank you that you love me so fully and with such abandon. Thank you that I can come to you and there is nothing I need to be ashamed of in your presence. Thank you that in you all is forgiven, accepted, and adored. Thank you that I am Your daughter, You are always with me, and that I am wrapped in Your love. I want to stay wrapped up in Your love, Lord.
Amen.

24.
Errand Day Prayer

. . . the Lord appeared to [her] from far away. I have loved you with an everlasting love; therefore I have continued my faithfulness to you.
Jeremiah 31:3

Hallelujah for still wearing my yoga pants and baseball cap this busy weekday at 1:30, eating an apple out of the Costco packaging for lunch, and doing my devotions in between picking kids up . . . in all of this greasy-hair-under-a-cap, stretching, heavy, busy, appointment-filled life, I know this one thing: He loves me. And He loves you. Be blessed today and know that you are enough. Amen.

Lord, help me to remember that it is in these busy, ordinary days that you are moving in my life. You delight in me even with my greasy hair I haven't had time to wash and you care about every detail of my life. I thank you that you move even in these errands and these chores with me, that I am never alone and never forgotten. I pray that I will bring you glory even in these small moments of my day.
Amen.

25.
Bless This Temple

You are altogether beautiful, my darling; there is no flaw in you.
Song of Solomon 4:7

One afternoon on vacation, Jack sent me to the pool to relax while the kids took a nap. As I settled down into my lawn chair, I didn't even think about how I looked in my swimsuit. After three babies in four years, bed rest, NICUs, and endless doctors' appointments, I couldn't have cared less what I looked like that blessed afternoon I spent by the pool alone. I ordered chips, guacamole, and a glass of wine and reveled in my naptime freedom. That is, until a young woman about seventeen sprawled her perky body across the lawn chair next to me.

She wasn't overly provocative or flirty, behaving no differently than I would have at her age. But she just was, ya know? that *fresh gorgeous* that turns heads.

I'm not a very jealous person by nature, but it was difficult to not start asking myself how in the world *Miss Fresh Gorgeous* turns into--well, to be honest--me. I sat there, remembering my own first bloom at seventeen, when I wasn't even sure of this gift of a body I'd been given. I had just stared in the mirror in shock over the way a bikini did, in fact, fit me.

As the afternoon progressed, I noticed how much my young and gorgeous counterpart fidgeted with her suit. She turned and readjusted herself, as if she was working out this new body of hers, like a new car she hadn't yet gotten comfortable driving. And while I wistfully admired and even envied her perky hot number that day at the pool, I didn't for one second wish to return to her phase of novice womanhood.

That night, while my family slept, I brushed my teeth in front of the mirror and stopped to look at myself for a good long while. I stared at my sunburned shoulders and my pore-pocked face, along with the new wrinkles starting to form from too much stress or just too many days by the pool. I tried not to focus on the lines running down the sides of my nose from the way I've always scrunched my face up to smile. I made a mental note to get home from vacation and buy wrinkle cream.

As I washed my face, I let my scrutiny fall to my hands. Sporting the same rings and holding the same man's hands every day for a good fifteen years, I failed to wear gloves or get manicures after washing mountains of dirty dishes and planting gardens. *You can tell by their wear.* Yet, they've served up love in countless meals and softed feverish heads, typed hundreds of blog posts, and folded thousands of loads of laundry.

And as I slipped on my pajamas, I couldn't help but wince. I sport more stretch marks from my lithium weight than my swelling humongous to deliver three babies. *And, oh, these legs!* I've had a love-hate relationship with them since girlhood. I've always wanted the other girls' skinny "chicken legs," to wear skinny jeans and look like something other than a stuffed turkey in them. But turkey or chicken, these legs have rocked me and my babies back and forth in Aunt Ginny's old glider, paced waiting room floors, and sprinted at the sound of my babies' cries. And I am grateful for them, to be carried through this life by sturdy and reliable *if not chicken* legs.

I don't know when it happened, but somehow between all the ways I've been angry at this precious, God-given body for failing me, all the ways I've punished her for falling short, I started to see all the ways I needed her and all

71

the ways she's come through for me. I started to cherish her for the temple she is, for the spirit of God she houses, not just for the sum of her parts (1 Corinthians 3:16). And when I started to see my body as temple--as sacred--I started to say thank you more and scrutinize less.

As I closed my eyes that night, I whispered to heaven, *I praise you because I am fearfully and wonderfully made*, not only in spirit, but in this body as well. I have been blessed with a precious temple in which I've loved a man, co-created children, fed, dressed, held, rocked, hugged, and danced. I have been blessed.

But I did hunt down that wrinkle cream when I got home . . .

Good luck at the pool, sisters!

Lord, I praise you for my miraculous body. Thank you for all the ways you allow me to experience the world, love my family, and live out my days in this temple. Help me to be a good steward with my body and always remember that it is a gift from You.
Amen.

26.
This Mother's Prayer

I want to be the mother
at the playground
who skips and puddle-jumps,
light enough on my feet
to scamper after my children,
playing joyful, singing silly.

I want to be the mom
in the grocery store
pushing the cart full of quiet kids
who aren't screaming for a cookie
or trying to escape
the screaming banshee they call *Mama*.

I want to be the mother who greets her children
everyday
    with a home-made cookie
    and a clean house
    and the smell of dinner on the stove
    and fresh laundry
    and a happy, excited, rested face
    and energy to tackle homework
    . . . and "mind your manners" . . .
    . . . and "just two more bites" . . .
    . . . and dishes,
    and bath-time, bedtime stories . . .
    . . . tooth-brush wrestling . . .

And I want to be the mama
who takes time to snuggle,
read the monkey story for the

35th night,
balancing a strict bedtime
with one more goodnight kiss.

And I want to be thin,
    svelte
        and sexy . . .
After all of the above!
I want to be the mother
    who loves her partner . . .
So they grow up to make
happy homes for their own families
and lasting love for themselves.

I want to know you, Lord,
    in the seconds I find alone
    and undistracted.
I want . . . to be PERFECT.
    Although I know I'm not.
And I long to love them all
the way You love me,
with patience and kindness
and an everlasting sense of humor.

So if I accomplish all of these things or none,
Help me to remember
That what I want to be
Can't compare to who I already am in You.
Amen.

27.
Reclaiming My Cinderella Heart

"Whatever comes," she said, "cannot alter one thing. If I
am a princess in rags and tatters, I can be a princess inside.
It would be easy to be a princess if I were dressed in cloth of
gold, but it is a great deal more of a triumph to be one all
the time when no one knows it."
— Frances Hodgson Burnett, A Little Princess

My mother stayed up all night to watch Lady Diana
marry Prince Charles. She loved the dress and the pomp,
like anyone. But what she recounted to me the next morning
at the breakfast table was not what Diana wore. Rather,
Mom noted Diana's elegance: the way she spoke, the way
she conducted herself, the way she treated others. I sat in
wonder for the rest of that day, watching clips of the
wedding alongside her, taking careful mental notes on what
a princess does and does not do.

Being a "princess" began early for me. My father
insisted that I was special, calling me "princess" from my
infancy. My mother insisted upon my royal heritage as well,
focusing on honing my character into that of royalty. She
defined this term "princess" almost strictly by behavior:
princesses do this, princesses don't do that.

Years later, we watched Princess Kate walking down
the same aisle as Diana. My mother, again, studied the way
the new royal carried herself. She whispered, "Her mother
must be so proud." So proud. I teared up remembering my
own wedding day, and how proud she was of me. I don't
know if I ever achieved the same level of elegance with a
cathedral length train covered in grass stains and frosting
and wine by the end of the evening. But I do remember
feeling like a princess.

Almost fifteen years later, my wedding dress lays balled up on the floor of my spare closet. After three babies, stretch marks, and the extra pounds they left behind, after the faded scars on my arms from depression so deep I didn't know what my razor was doing, after grief that hung around my neck for so long it left me feeling old and worn out, I watched that royal princess in disbelief.

I realized I hardly could remember what it felt like to be a princess. I realized that somewhere in the storm, when the waves started crashing, when I couldn't keep my head above the water, somehow sadness gave way to shame, and I lost my princess identity. In all of the hurt and the brokenness of those years, I lost myself. And I wanted my princess heart back.

Lately, we've been watching a lot of Disney's cartoon version of Cinderella in our house. My boys love the mice, especially Jack-Jack and Gus-Gus. But I watch her. I watch her scrubbing floors out of the corner of my eye while I'm scrubbing dishes. I watch her kindness toward the animals as I try to patiently sweep under the kids' table for the 50th time this week. I watch her endure the harshness of her stepmother and stepsisters. I watch her when she discovers that every maiden in the kingdom is invited to Prince Charming's ball. And I watch as she does not hesitate for one moment in her belief that she belongs at that ball.

Now, I know Cinderella is a cartoon, but bear with me here: wouldn't you hesitate? She lost her parents, her wealth, and all social standing. She was stripped of her title as lady of the castle and forced to be the maid. She was subjugated, reviled, and held captive for years. And, yet, in the midst of years of tragedy and abuse, Cinderella never let go of the truth she held deep in her heart: she was a princess.

So, when her prince came knocking, Cinderella was ready. She didn't care if she was wearing a decades-old hand-me-down dress trimmed out by mice. She was confident in the fact that she was royalty, and she belonged at the palace. She never allowed her circumstances to change her value.

Looking back, I can see where I lost sight of the fact that I, too, am a princess. I can look back at the day I gave up on being royal, of being special. How could anyone special, royal, be broken down by life this many times? Where was the fairness, where was the King? Is He in charge, or is this just some big, cosmic joke? After all of my failings, all of my sin, all of my brokenness, I forgot I had a place in the Palace with my name on it. I forgot I even belonged there.

Are you there? Has life hammered the princess out of you? Are you in a hospital room right now, wearing faded yoga pants for the 700th day in a row? Are you so tired you don't even care what you look like anymore? Are you chained to a bed in a psyche ward drugged out of your mind, trying on a new diagnosis? Are you moving back in with your parents after your marriage blew apart? Are you so broken open that nothing—no one—could ever make you whole again?

Yes, I know, sister. I've been all those things. And I stopped believing that I was anything special. I stopped believing I deserved good anymore. I stopped believing life could be better. It was just too torturous to hope anymore.

But what the TRUTH is, sister, is this: these broken moments in hospital rooms late at night, these mornings when you just don't know how you're going to make it until noon, these days where you're covered in so many bodily fluids you can't keep count, these afternoons where you have lost who you are in the needs and caring for others—

These are Cinderella moments.

These are the moments when a whole new batch of

queens are being made, refined, and purified. These are the moments when being royal becomes a job description instead of just a title. These are the moments when you grab on to your Godly heritage and you affirm:

I am the daughter of the King. "I will be a Father to you, and you will be my sons and daughters, says the Lord Almighty" (2 Corinthians 6:18).

My father delights in me. "The LORD your God is with you, the Mighty Warrior who saves. He will take great delight in you; in his love he will no longer rebuke you, but will rejoice over you with singing"
(Zephaniah 3:17).

My father defines my worth. "See what great love the Father has lavished on us, that we should be called children of God! And that is what we are! The reason the world does not know us is that it did not know him"
(1 John 3:1).

He defines my beauty by the content of my character (not the spit-up on my t-shirt, my faded yoga pants, my tired eyes and grown-out hair cut, not the scars on my arms, or the 100 extra pounds I'm wearing, my shiny chemo'd scalp, or the puffed up lithium look I'm sporting.) "Your beauty should not come from outward adornment, such as elaborate hairstyles and the wearing of gold jewelry or fine clothes. Rather, it should be that of your inner self, the unfading beauty of a gentle and quiet spirit, which is of great worth in God's sight"(1 Peter 3:3-4).

He will never leave me or forsake me. "Behold, I am with you and will keep you wherever you go, and will bring you back to this land; for I will not leave you until I have done what I have promised you" (Genesis 28:15).

He will never stop working for my good. "And I will make an everlasting covenant with them: I will never stop doing good for them. I will put a desire in their hearts to worship me, and they will never leave me" (Jeremiah 32:40).

His deepest desire is to bring me home to Him, to live forever as his beloved. "As a young man marries a young woman, so will your Builder marry you; as a bridegroom rejoices over his bride, so will your God rejoice over you" (Isaiah 62:5).

He says I am Very Good. Period (Genesis 1:31). That is the truth of who you are. It doesn't matter what you've done or what's been done to you. It doesn't matter who you've hurt, or if they ever forgive you. It doesn't matter the sin, the disease, the condition, the station you've been wearing as your self-description. You and I are daughters of the king, and our rightful place is in the castle.

So wherever you are today, do not stop believing for one moment that your rightful place is with the King. Never stop believing that you are a true princess. No matter how long it takes for your circumstances to change, the fact that you are loved never falters. Hold your head high today, sister. One day you'll be queen.

Lord, restore me. Restore my vision of myself. Help me to see myself the way You see me, help me to see all the gifts and possibilities I still possess. Revive the Cinderella in my heart. Amen.

I trust You, Lord,
to give every moment of my life--
every pain,
every strength and weakness,
every gift--
purpose and meaning
so that I may see
my life overflow
for my best good
and the good of others.
Amen

28.
Just One More Request

Then Gideon said to God, "Do not be angry with me. Let me make just one more request. Allow me one more test with the fleece, but this time make the fleece dry and let the ground be covered with dew." That night God did so. Only the fleece was dry; all the ground was covered with dew.
Judges 6:39-40

Imagine Gideon's fear. When Gideon's angel appeared to him, he was hiding in a winepress threshing wheat to keep it safe from the Midianites. The angel said, "The Lord is with you, mighty warrior." But something about his hiding in the winepress act tells me Gideon might not have been so mighty. Maybe he was a bit more like me and you, just caught up in the day to day of surviving and finding out where the party was going to be on Saturday night. Maybe he wasn't thinking a whole lot about leading his people to victory or getting out of bondage from foreign gods.

When Gideon realizes that the Lord is choosing him to lead the charge, his words sound a whole lot like mine might have, "Pardon me, my lord . . . but how can I save Israel? My clan is the weakest . . . and I am the least in my family."

I am the least.

And what does the Lord reply?

"I will be with you . . ."

But as Gideon began to piece together the minutiae of God's plan—to raise an army and fight the dreaded Midianites–can't you see him just shaking his head? Even if he truly believed God would be with him? At every turn, he must have questioned his own sanity. At every new step forward, he must have needed new assurances. But then again, don't we all?

I tend to think of God as a general: He gives the orders, and His minions are supposed to follow. But, I'm learning very slowly that that's not how He works at all. He cares deeply that the work we do outside of ourselves reflects the work being done within us. He's not in the business of pouring us out until we're empty. Instead, He's filling us from the inside out so that we naturally overflow. He's not going to get angry with us if we keep coming to Him like Gideon did. Every time I return to God for reassurance, He bolsters me. He prepares me. He fills me up.

So even if you wonder how you can ever ask for too much reassurance from your Heavenly Father, you can't. Even when you're certain He'll just turn you away, ask. And even when you should be filled up, but you're not? Ask again. Just keep asking. Keep going back. He's in the business of filling. He's ready and willing to fill you to overflowing so when your day of battle comes, you're ready. Keep on asking until you feel ready. Keep on asking until you're flooded with the assurance that can only come from Him. Go on, Gideon-heart. Ask.

Lord, please give me a Gideon heart with boldness to ask again and again for the reassurance I need from you to be filled and filled and filled again with all the love and kindness only you can give. The only place I can get the filling I need to do the work you've commissioned me to do in the world is from Your throne; please help me to never forget it.
Amen.

29.
A Different Purpose

For a long time,
i prayed for purpose.
i envisioned dress up clothes
& high heels.
importance.
my name in print.
i asked for destiny,
use of my talents,
education, skill.

Then, God laid you in my arms.
A Fatherly whisper:
"Hold this for a while."
My body battered--
head-to-toe in bruise and tape—
my weary eyes squinted
at your puffy, drugged up face.
i reached for you;
Your tiny body all flinch in pain.
"It's the meds," they said.

i understood: meds.
i understood a body flooded
with poison to save a life.
i understood.
So i found a pillow and sat down.
They placed you in my arms,
 into your place beneath my heart:
drugged, poisoned, alive.
i stared at the walls and sang to you,
my tears choking,

my heart beating my deepest fears.

Now, two years spent,
i hold you still.
You lean against my chest
still listening for my heart.
Your puffed up lips and swollen hands
beg for a relief I cannot give you.
i hold you still.
in the black of night—
Zipper scar and med reactions—
blood draws and x-rays.
My heartbeat
harbors you from horror.

These days stretch out
And i wonder when you and i
Will move freely into the world as two hearts:
You healthy and strong,
me with something else to beat for.
But for today and endless days,
i surrender as the wine offering poured out
upon the altar of your life.
i am the beat, the hope, the love
God fashioned to guide you through.
i pulse to carry you down this road.

As long as i live,
my destiny lies in yours.
We share singular purpose in
moving you forward in life.
We share destiny
walking this road together.
We share drugs, poison, courage.

We persist.
We share the beat of my heart
The grit that moves us onward,
the love that fights for you.

30.
When Your Angel Comes

In the sixth month of Elizabeth's pregnancy, God sent the angel Gabriel to Nazareth, a town in Galilee, to a virgin pledged to be married to a man named Joseph, a descendant of David. The virgin's name was Mary. The angel went to her and said, "Greetings, you who are highly favored! The Lord is with you."

Mary was greatly troubled at his words and wondered what kind of greeting this might be. But the angel said to her, "Do not be afraid, Mary; you have found favor with God. You will conceive and give birth to a son, and you are to call him Jesus. He will be great and will be called the Son of the Most High. The Lord God will give him the throne of his father David, and he will reign over Jacob's descendants forever; his kingdom will never end."

"How will this be," Mary asked the angel, "since I am a virgin?"

The angel answered, "The Holy Spirit will come on you, and the power of the Most High will overshadow you. So the holy one to be born will be called the Son of God. Even Elizabeth your relative is going to have a child in her old age, and she who was said to be unable to conceive is in her sixth month. For no word from God will ever fail."

"I am the Lord's servant," Mary answered. "May your word to me be fulfilled." Then the angel left her.
Luke 1: 26-38

There is a refrain being sung all over the world by mothers who have been given more than any human being was ever meant to bear. There is a prayer being whispered on a million mamas' lips:
Where do I find the strength?

I prayed and wailed and screamed this over and over again to God when I was pregnant with Samuel. With every step we took on the journey alongside him, with every sleepless hour in the night, with every morning's dawn, every doctor's appointment and every test, I prayed, "please help me to find the strength." I was convinced that God had chosen the wrong woman, the wrong time in my life. I was too broken already, too weakened. I had already seen too much, buried too much, survived too much for this journey. And what if I just couldn't do it? What if I cracked under the pressure, what if I ended up in the nut house? What of my children then?

I thought a lot about that moment when Mary's world turned upside down. I wondered at the likelihood that she would have been taken to a mental hospital in today's world had she returned from a stay at her aunt's house with a big, pregnant belly and the unlikely story of Gabriel's visitation. I wondered, as I walked a breath-by-breath existence, how she walked hers: this child, this unmarried virgin mother, this pleaser of God. I wondered if she cried every day when no one was looking, if she was scared to be alone with this God-child growing inside of her, if she was afraid the angel would come back or afraid he would never show his face again.

And as I groped through the darkness of my own terrifying pregnancy, I learned two things Mary must have learned, too:

1) He is not afraid of my smallness, and 2) even the dark is not darkness to Him. I didn't need to put on a brave face to do the brave thing. I didn't need to play holy. I only needed to answer, "Here am I, the servant of the Lord; let it be with me according to your word" (Luke 1:38).

We all get stuck on the hows of following God's calling on our lives, and the hows are never the real question. The real question is always will you?

Yes. I will. And I'm going to screw this up most days. I'm going to scream and throw things at the wall. I'm going to self-medicate and falter and wake up the next morning determined to do better. I'm going to hold grudges and think people should help more, all the while forgetting to ask God for help. I'm going to do this as humanly, error-ridden, and awkwardly as possible.

And I'm also going to have moments where the angels come, and the grace pours in, moments of pure joy, moments where I see His face.

And I am going to keep saying yes. And I am going to keep asking for forgiveness and strength and grace in every breath. Because I know now that every breath is derived from You. And in my human yes, I am forever tied to You.

Just say yes, friend. The strength will come on angels' wings, as the tide is going out, and on the crest of the incoming waves. He will give and give and give to You. And You will learn to walk the darkness with a heart full of hope and a light in your heart. You will learn to hold angels' hands, to see with faith-sight, to receive the greatest gifts heaven pours into earth, saved always for the mamas screaming their prayers to sky.

You will find your strength, friend. You will find it.

For nothing is impossible with God (Luke 1:37).

Lord, give me the strength to trust you into the darkness of pure calling. Give me the courage to follow you into deep ocean where only your Spirit can sustain me. I know that there is nowhere you can lead me where you will not protect and nourish my heart. I trust you with my family, my marriage, my home, and my fear. I give you my dreams. I'm all in.

Amen.

31.
What You'd Never Dare To Ask

They will rebuild the ancient ruins and restore the places long devastated; they will renew the ruined cities that have been devastated for generations.
Isaiah 61:4

As I walked along the wet wooden planks of Malibu Club the first morning of Women's Weekend, the sound of worship gently fell upon my still waking ears. The notes carried through my body as they had done throughout my childhood and teen years in so many camps on so many early mornings just like this one, the memories flooding through me like a download of harmonious lightness. I stood there, soaking in the feelings of a hundred praise song memories, of campfires and early morning bible studies. My whole body quaked with joy, as in a deep remembrance, as if some sleeping part of me revived back to life: an old girlhood, rapturous, unbroken happiness. And I started to feel it, that real down deep aliveness, for the first time in so long I wanted to stand there in the rain and weep, to remember her.

I found bits of her all weekend long, collecting her in the coffee shop as I wrote in my journal and watching the seals as I prayed. I found her in the seminars as I took careful notes and in the dance party, bouncing up and down, shouting YMCA. By the end of the weekend I'd discovered so many pieces of her that I realized she wouldn't fit in my suitcase. I would have to carry her with me. But that's okay. See, I really don't want to lose her again.

Life has a way of stripping us of our sparkle, of ripping out our joy. I lost my fire, my childhood dream girl who loved camp and seals and putting her toes in the water at night. But our God is so big He gives it all back, sister. He doesn't just save us. He gives our sparkle back. And then He gives back the things we never even think to ask for, the things so long devastated and forgotten only He can remember to revive them. That was how I felt that weekend at Malibu: like God took the care to restore my places long devastated, the places I didn't think could ever be put back together again.

I have always prayed for the big things in my life for God to reassemble, but not the small things. But He never forgets about the small things. He remembers the details. When I stop to really think about it, I've realized that it's the small things that have mattered the most in restoring my soul. Being able to go to camp and do Bible study and praise and worship restored something so deep in my heart I had no idea it was even missing. But He knew.

And He will do that for you. He will give back your dreams, the secret things you can't even begin to ask for. He will restore your heart like He keeps restoring mine. So come pray with me today,

Big God, I'm asking that you will restore my heart. Life is hard, Lord, and I feel like it is easy to always ask for the big things and so easy to forget to ask you just to tend my heart. I want back that joy and sparkle I used to have. Will you restore in me the dreams and hopes I dared to dream when I was younger? I trust in you to not just save me, but to renew me.
Amen.

My Prayer For You

For I know the plans I have for you," declares the Lord, "plans to prosper you and not to harm you, plans to give you hope and a future.
Jeremiah 29:11

Wherever you find yourself in this moment, whether in the backyard under the soaring sky with the warm earth squishing between your toes, or scrunched inside a fluorescent-lit cubicle typing up your tenth report, I pray purpose finds you here. Yes, friend, true purpose. I know the lie of the world can slither in so close, up around your neck, and whisper so loud that the only purpose you think you can accomplish in this world is something grand and noteworthy and shiny. But that is a lie. Every day you live and breathe and love in this world, every day you push forward, is a trophy-making day. Every act of love, every choice for another, is an accomplishment in your Father's eyes.

You are Abba's girl. You have purpose because you are His. Every time you laugh, every time you open your heart up to love, your purpose is revealed in this world. You are here to love and be loved, to experience God's creation, to know what it is to be a child of God. All the rest will come in time.

So when you're sitting at that desk wondering why you're working a job that strangles you when all you want to do is be at home with your kids, ask Him. He will show you purpose. When you're homebound with a brood of children, desperate for reprieve, ask Him, He'll show you purpose. When you feel sandwiched between caring for your aging parents and your children, overwhelmed with responsibility, ask Him to show you the meaning of it all. Just a glimpse.

I often find in the midst of the chaotic and frustrating

times, when all I want to do is make a little sense of my life that keeping a journal helps tremendously. If I am asking for direction, and especially for purpose, practicing the spiritual exercise, the Examen, in my journal helps me. The Examen asks three questions:

1. What brought me life today?
2. What took life from me today?
3. What grace can I ask for for tomorrow?

As I record what brings me life and what does not, I can see God working in my life. God purposes those life-giving things and the life-taking things whether I realize it or not; it just takes a little practice for me to see it. Patterns begin to emerge as I record my daily Examen reflections.

If you watch these patterns develop in your journal over a period of time, you will see clear directions from the Holy Spirit about whatever your heart needs to hear. All of my major life decisions have been determined while practicing the Examen.

My prayer for you is that wherever you are in your life that you see God working. I pray that you see your life as purpose-filled, whether your paycheck is filled with zeroes or lots of dirty diapers and slobbery kisses. Know this: you are loved beyond measure and you are the daughter of the King. Nothing, nothing can ever take that away from you. Be blessed, my dear friend. Please come say hello over on my website, TaylorKArthur.com. I would love to hear from you.

With so much love,

Taylor

ABOUT THE AUTHOR

Taylor K. Arthur writes and speaks about living free with
bipolar disorder, marriage, and motherhood inspired by a
grace-soaked faith in a God who refuses to let her go.
Her favorite place in the world is her back porch in Puyallup,
WA, surrounded by her family and friends and dear neighbors
as they drop by. You can visit her at her online home,
taylorkarthur.com.

Made in the USA
Lexington, KY
21 November 2019